Investigating settlements

Caroline Clissold

Heinemann
LIBRARY

www.heinemann.co.uk/library
Visit our website to find out more information about **Heinemann Library** books.

To order:
☎ Phone 44 (0) 1865 888066
▤ Send a fax to 44 (0) 1865 314091
💻 Visit the Heinemann Bookshop at www.heinemann.co.uk/library to browse our catalogue and order online.

First published in Great Britain by Heinemann Library, Halley Court, Jordan Hill, Oxford OX2 8EJ, part of Harcourt Education. Heinemann is a registered trademark of Harcourt Education Ltd.

© Harcourt Education Ltd 2006
The moral right of the proprietor has been asserted.

Editorial: Vicki Yates
Design: Dave Poole and Tokay Interactive Limited (www.tokay.co.uk)
Illustrations: Geoff Ward and International Mapping (www.internationalmapping.com)
Picture Research: Hannah Taylor
Production: Duncan Gilbert

Originated by Repro Multi Warna
Printed in China by WKT Company Limited

10 digit ISBN: 0 431 03253 X   (Hardback)
13 digit ISBN: 978 0 431 03253 5 (Hardback)
10 09 08 07 06
10 9 8 7 6 5 4 3 2 1

10 digit ISBN: 0 431 03260 2   (Paperback)
13 digit ISBN: 978 0 431 03260 3 (Paperback)
10 09 08 07 06
10 9 8 7 6 5 4 3 2 1

British Library Cataloguing in Publication Data
Clissold, Caroline
Investigating settlements
910.9 ' 1734
A full catalogue record for this book is available from the British Library.

Acknowledgements
The publishers would like to thank the following for permission to reproduce photographs:
Action Aid p. **25**, Alamy Images p. **21** (G P Bowater), p. **22** (Hugh Williamson), p. **24** (Marc Hill), p. **26** (Photofusion Picture Library); Corbis p. **6** (Chris Andrews; Chris Andrews Publications), p. **8** (Jan Butchofsky-Houser), p. **15** (Bob Krist), p. **29** (Jeremy Horner); Getty Images p. **5** (Hulton Archive), pp. **9b, 28** (Stone); Harcourt Education p. **16** (Tudor Photography); Hutchinson Picture Library pp. **19, 23, 27** (Liba Taylor); Reproduced by permission of Ordnance Survey on behalf of The Controller of Her Majesty's Stationery Office, © Crown Copyright 100000230 pp. **7, 9t**, **10**, **11t, 11b, 14**; Skyscan pp. **12, 13**, p. **4** (LAPL).

Cover photograph of a road through a housing development, reproduced with permission of Corbis/Jason Hawkes.

The publishers would like to thank Rebecca Harman, Rachel Bowles, Robyn Hardyman, and Caroline Landon for their assistance in the preparation of this book.

Every effort has been made to contact copyright holders of any material reproduced in this book. Any omissions will be rectified in subsequent printings if notice is given to the publishers.

All the Internet addresses (URLs) given in this book were valid at the time of going to press. However, due to the dynamic nature of the Internet, some addresses may have changed, or sites may have changed or ceased to exist since publication. While the author and Publishers regret any inconvenience this may cause readers, no responsibility for any such changes can be accepted by either the author or the Publishers.

Exploring further

Throughout this book you will find links to the Heinemann Explore CD-ROM and website at www.heinemannexplore.com. Follow the links to find out more about the topic.

Contents

Any words appearing in the text in bold, **like this**, are explained in the glossary.

What are settlements?

Most people live in a **settlement**, like a **city** or a **town**. This means they live in one place. When we study geography we can find out who first lived in a place and why and how it developed to become a **village**, town or city.

Imagine you are moving to a new area, what would you need to have first? Most importantly you need to have a roof over your head, somewhere to buy food and clothes, and perhaps access to a good school.

Thousands of years ago, things were not too different for the people who settled in your area. They had the same basic needs as we do: somewhere sheltered from extreme **weather**, land and materials for building their shelters, woodland for safety, flat land for growing crops, and fresh, clean water for drinking.

Where did early settlers choose to settle?

On a map of the UK you will find that many towns and cities are next to rivers. Many of these places are settlements from the past that have grown into what they are today because they are beside a river. Early settlers chose these locations because they could take the water they needed from the rivers. Some examples of these places include: London on the River Thames; Newcastle on the River Tyne; and Bristol on the River Avon.

■ Look in an **atlas** to find out which river the city of Durham in northern England is located next to. Using this photograph, can you think why this would have been a good place for a settlement?

Who were some of the early settlers?

Most settlements in the UK were started by the Celts, the Romans, the Anglo-Saxons, and the Vikings, over a thousand years ago. The Celts were early settlers. They lived in **fortified** settlements on the tops of hills, or in small villages or farms.

The Romans came from Rome, now the capital of Italy. They had an enormous empire across Europe and wanted to make Britain a part of it. They invaded Britain in AD 43.

The name Anglo-Saxon is given to a group of several peoples from northern Europe (Angles, Saxons, and Jutes) who invaded Britain between the 5th and 7th centuries.

Vikings lived in large parts of Scandinavia. They traded with – and raided – much of Europe, and often settled there. They began to raid the UK in 793.

■ *The Vikings travelled from Scandinavia to the UK by boat.*

Exploring further

On the Heinemann Explore website or CD-ROM go to Exploring > Seaside resorts. Read the article on St Ives. Look at the photographs and maps that go with it. Watch the video 'The harbour in St Ives'. Think about why people would have settled there.

How can we identify early settlements?

Using place names

The beginnings or endings of place names can often tell us about the origins of **villages**, **towns** and **cities**, for example, who settled there and what the land was like. Below you can see some of the most common beginnings and endings of place names that were introduced by early settlers in Britain.

Celtic place names

avon, afon – river
lan, llan – church
tre, tref – house or farm
tor – hill

Viking place names

by – farm or village
thorp, thorpe – farm or small village
kirk – church
ness – headland

Anglo-Saxon place names

borough, bury, brough, burgh – **fortified** place
wick, wich – farm
ham – homestead, village, or **water meadow**
ton, tun – **enclosure**, farm, or village
stead, sted – place

Roman place names

cester, caster, chester – fort or town
coln – settlement
port – gate or harbour

■ *The place name Stratford-upon-Avon tells us that the town of Stratford is located on a river, in this case the River Avon, and that Celts were the first people to settle there.*

The name of a **settlement** often gives an indication of what that settlement was like in the past. For example, Inverness had a **headland** and Warwick was an area of farmland. How do you think these settlements might have changed since they were given their names?

Activity

1 Write down the names of the villages on the map below that show evidence of an early settlement.

2 Explain how the name provides a clue to who the early settlers were.

3 Can you think of any reasons why each village was an attractive site for early settlers.

© Crown Copyright

How can we identify Roman settlements?

One of the most well-known settlements in the UK that was invaded by the Romans was the city of Colchester in Essex. The names of many Roman settlements ended with '-ester'. If you look at a map you will find that many British towns and cities have this ending. This is often because they have Roman origins. For example, Chichester, Leicester, Manchester, Gloucester, Worcester, and Chester were all Roman settlements. Other important Roman settlements included York, London, and St Albans.

Activity

Think about the Roman town of Bath and see if you can work out why the Romans chose it as a settlement. Draw a map of the town centre and show all the evidence of Roman settlement you can find. The Internet may help you carry out this task.

How can we identify Anglo-Saxon settlements?

The Angles settled mostly in East Anglia, Mercia (central England), and Northumbria. The Saxons settled in Essex, Sussex, and Wessex (on the south-east coast of England).

The names of towns and cities with Anglo-Saxon origins often end with '-ton'. Here are some examples: Surbiton, Kingston, and Littlehampton. If you look at these places on a map you will find they are all in areas where the Anglo-Saxons settled.

- *How many Anglo-Saxon settlements can you find on this map of part of Surrey?*

How can we identify Viking settlements?

Viking rule began first in Scotland and parts of Ireland. The Vikings also took control of most of the Anglo-Saxon kingdoms in England, an area known as the Danelaw. The names of towns and cities with Viking origins often end with '-by', for example Enderby, Derby, Selby, and Sowerby.

- *Whitby in Yorkshire was a Viking settlement. This is the town today.*

Activity

1 List as many UK towns and cities as you can that end in '-ester'.

2 List as many UK towns and cities as you can that end in '-ton'.

3 List as many UK towns and cities as you can that end in '-by'.

4 Now use an **atlas** to find all the places you have listed.

What evidence of settlements can we find on maps?

In geography, maps can help us to find evidence of settlers in the UK. Maps can also help to explain why people actually chose to settle in that area. Below and on the next page are some examples of early settlements.

Norfolk

If you look at Ordnance Survey maps of the area around Norfolk you will notice that there are many **towns** and **villages** whose names end with '-ham'. These include Taverham, Dereham, Swaftham, Shipham, and Hindringham. There are also a few with other endings, for example '-ton', such as Brampton and Hempton.

Leicester

The east midlands town of Leicester was a Roman settlement, we can tell this because of the ending '-ester'. The Vikings then moved in. We can tell this by looking at a map of the **outskirts** of Leicester. There are many towns whose names end in '-by', such as Groby and Enderby. These are Viking names.

- '-ham' is a common place name ending in this part of Norfolk. What do you think that shows us? Who do you think were the original settlers in this area?

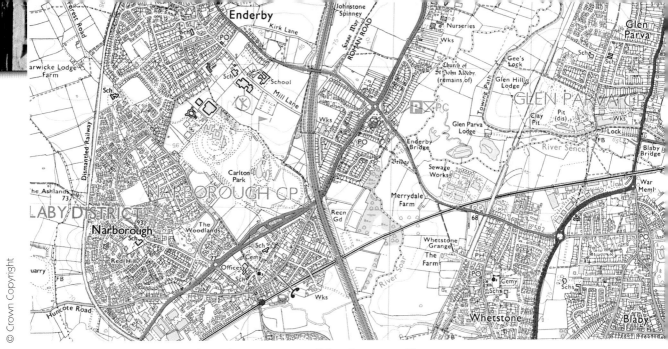

■ *The places whose names end in '-by' were once Viking farms or villages.*

Northumberland

We can also find out a lot by looking at maps of the area north-west of Newcastle-upon-Tyne. Here, there are many places with names ending with '-ton'. These **settlements** are all located near rivers in areas that are not likely to flood. They are also located in areas of flat land that would have been good for farming.

■ *This map of the area around Newcastle-upon-Tyne shows some places with names ending in '-ton'. What does this tell us about them?*

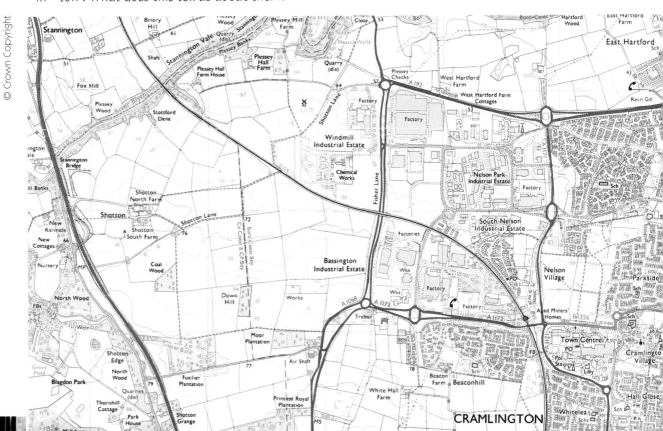

How do settlements develop?

All **settlements** have special features. They often developed in the places that they did because of the **physical features** of the **landscape**, for example near rivers because the settlers needed water.

If you look at a settlement on a map or an **aerial photograph**, you may be able to see why it has developed where it has. Think about how any physical features of the landscape have influenced the settlement, such as rivers or flat land. Also think about the **human features**, such as the availability of housing, shops and schools.

■ *This is the town of Warkworth in Northumberland. You can clearly see how the town has grown up around the curve of the river.*

Choosing a site

The early settlers chose their land very carefully. They asked themselves some of these questions:

- Is there a supply of fresh water, like a river, so that we can drink?
- Is there any flat land for farming?
- Is there a sheltered place for protection against bad **weather**?
- Do we need to be on a hill to protect us against any enemies?

Settlement size

A settlement can be any size. One farm is a settlement. It is called an **isolated settlement**. A settlement that is made up of just a few houses is called a **hamlet**. When there are more houses and services, like a pub or a post office, it is called a **village**.

■ *The early settlers in Ironbridge in Shropshire would have chosen this site because it is next to a river. You can see that the settlement then grew along the river, so it is long and thin. The opposite bank of the river is still wooded, because it was too steep for people to build houses on.*

Activity

1 Imagine you are moving to a new settlement. You have found a site with a river that runs through it.
2 What else would you like to have in your settlement?
3 Where you would want all these features to be?
4 How would you like your settlement to be connected to the areas around it?
5 Draw a map showing your settlement and give it a **key**.

Exploring further

Read the Exploring article on the city of Liverpool on the Heinemann Explore website or CD-ROM, and watch the video 'The Albert Docks in Liverpool'. These will show you how Liverpool developed as a settlement. Think about how the physical features of the landscape shaped its development, and why people would have wanted to settle there.

What are villages like today?

We can learn a lot about what a **village** is like today by looking at maps and interpreting the symbols on them.

Symbols on maps

If you look at a **rural** area on an Ordnance Survey map, you may see some small villages, but there are no large **towns** or **cities**. You will see symbols on the map that represent certain features, such as **nature reserves**, churches, railway lines, level crossings, buildings, roads and rivers.

When we know what these symbols mean, we can work out what a place is like just from looking at a map. We can see if there are certain types of buildings, such as a church or a post office. We can also see how this place is connected to other places, for example by roads, or railway.

Activity

1 Look at the Ordnance Survey map below.
2 See if you can you work out what the symbols mean before you look at the **key**.

■ *This is part of the Ordnance Survey map of Chipping Campden in Gloucestershire and the surrounding area.*

KEY

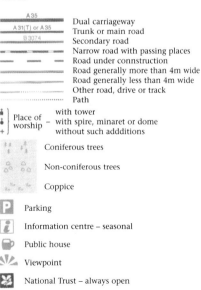

A 35   Dual carriageway
A 31(T) or A 35   Trunk or main road
B 3074   Secondary road
        Narrow road with passing places
        Road under connstruction
        Road generally more than 4m wide
        Road generally less than 4m wide
        Other road, drive or track
        Path

Place of worship – with tower
        with spire, minaret or dome
        without such addditions

        Coniferous trees

        Non-coniferous trees

        Coppice

P Parking

i Information centre – seasonal

☕ Public house

🔆 Viewpoint

❋ National Trust – always open

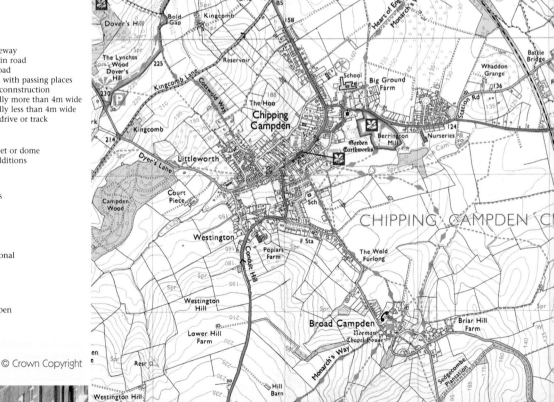

■ *Chipping Campden is a village in a rural setting.*

Comparing places

Still looking at the map, we can compare the village of Chipping Campden with a village near where you live. Which place is bigger, the village near you or Chipping Campden? Chipping Campden is close to a river and has road links to other areas. What about your local village? With a partner, make a list of the **physical features** and the **human features** of the village near you and Chipping Campden.

Exploring further

On the Heinemann Explore website or CD-ROM go to Exploring > Villages. Read the articles on Marconi Beam in South Africa. Think about how it might be similar or different to a village near you.

How are isolated settlements connected to villages?

If you lived in an **isolated settlement**, for example on a farm, it would be important for you to be connected to larger places, such as **villages** or **towns**. You would need to be able to get to shops to buy clothing and food. You would also need to be able to get to a doctor or a hospital if you were ill.

Roads, railways, and rivers

If you look at a map you will see that all settlements are connected to other settlements. Some are connected in a variety of ways, such as by roads, a railway, and a river, while others are connected by only one of these routes.

Activity

1 Think of reasons why a village like Chipping Campden in Gloucestershire would need to be connected to a larger town.

2 Make a list of all the different ways in which places can be connected to each other.

▪ *Chipping Campden is connected to the town of Evesham by a road.*

Using grid references

We are often helped to find places on maps by their **grid references**. In the map below, the lines going up (vertically) have letters and the lines going across (horizontally) have numbers. A grid reference tells you which square a feature is in. To give a grid reference, you give the number on the vertical line first and then the number on the horizontal line. For example in the map below you can find the school in G.4.

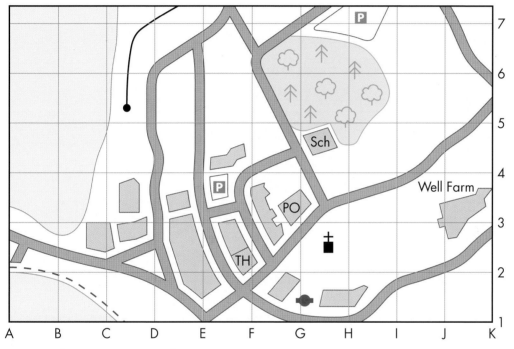

■ *Grid references help us to find places on maps quickly.*

So why are grid references so useful? You can use them to tell someone where a certain road is on a map. You could give them the grid reference of where it starts and the one for where it ends. Or you can give them the grid reference of a village or town.

Exploring further

On the Heinemann Explore website or CD-ROM go to Exploring > Villages. Read the exploring article 'A village called La Trinidad – physical aspects' and look at the map that goes with it. Draw a map to show its location and think about how it is connected to the places around it.

Chembakolli – a village in India

Finding the village

In geography we study other parts of the world that are different to ours. You can find lots of information about different places from **secondary sources** such as reference books, **atlases**, maps, photographs, and the Internet. Using this information you can compare your own **settlement** with the places that you study.

Locating a place in another country

The easiest way to find a place is to look at a globe, map, or atlas. Once you have your map or globe, how do you locate the place you are looking for? You need to start big! Do you know which **continent** it is on? When you have found the continent, work down from there. Which country is it in? Now think about where in the country it is. Do you know any major **cities** or **towns** that it is near? If you are using an atlas, you can look in the index to find the page and the **grid reference** for the location.

Where is Chembakolli?

Chembakolli is a small village in southern India. India is in the continent of Asia. Asia is next to the continent of Europe, which is where the UK is located.

■ *This world map shows where Chembakolli is and also where the UK is.*

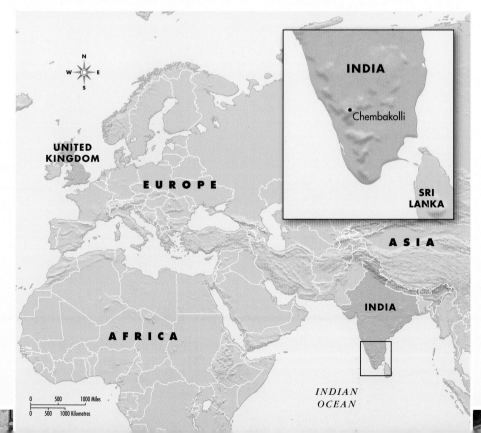

■ *Chembakolli is a small village in the hills to the south west of the city of Bangalore in southern India.*

Activity

1 Using your atlas, find out the following things about India:
 • which seas border it
 • the name of the **capital city**
 • which major river is in the north
 • which mountain range is in the north
 • what the climate is like.

2 Draw your own map of India, labelling the main **physical** and **human features**.

How is it connected to other places?

In geography, it is often easier to understand where a place is by thinking about its location in relation to other places. For example, India is on the **continent** of Asia. It is south of Nepal and China, east of Pakistan, and west of Bangladesh. We can use maps and **atlases** to help us find all these places and see how they are connected to each other.

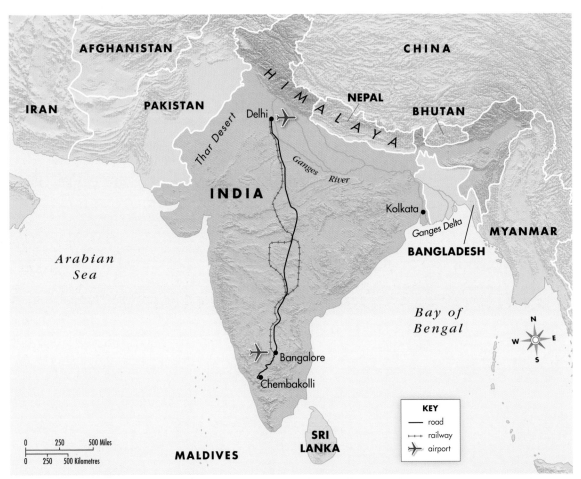

■ *This map of India shows how Chembakolli is connected to other places in India.*

Activity

1. Think about how you would get to India from the UK.
2. Use an atlas to plan your route.
3. Make a note of the countries you would travel across, the distance travelled, and the airports you would use (or perhaps you might travel by boat!)

How do I get to Chembakolli?

When you got to India, you would need to think about how you could get to Chembakolli. You would have to ask yourself the following questions:

- Which direction should I travel in?
- How far away is it?
- Could I fly to an airport nearby?
- Could I take the train there?

To answer these questions you need to find out about the area around Chembakolli. Look at pictures and maps of it. Are there roads, rivers, railways, or even an airport there?

There is an airport in Bangalore so you could fly there from Delhi. You could also travel by train or by road, but this would take much longer. When you get to Bangalore you would need to take a five hour train journey to Mysore, followed by a four hour bus journey to Gudalur. After all this time you would still need to travel by jeep for an hour to reach Chembakolli.

Once you get into the hills around Chembakolli there may only be dirt roads. In the rainy season these roads may turn into rivers of mud, so the bus may get stuck along the way. All these factors would make your journey to such a remote place a very long and difficult one.

■ *Transport in India can be very different from transport in the UK. Think about how this would affect your journey.*

What is the landscape like?

In geography, to fully understand the different ways that people live it is important to study the **landscape** around them.

Physical features

The **physical features** of the landscape have a direct effect on how people live. For example, if an area has lots of fertile land it is likely that people will use it for farming.

Human features

The **human features** are everything in the landscape made by humans. Homes, schools, factories, parks, and leisure facilities are all human features. Human features tell us about the ways that people live.

Human features are often affected by physical features. For example, the materials that buildings are made of will depend on what is available locally. If there is a large forest nearby, the houses may be made of wood. If the area is very flat, roads might form good transport links. If the area is surrounded by water, transport links are more likely to be by boat.

What is the landscape of India like?

India has a varied landscape. There are the Himalayas to the north and wild flower-filled highlands in the east. Other interesting areas include the western coastal lowlands, the Thar **Desert,** and the **mangrove** swamps of the River Ganges **delta**. How do you think these types of landscape would affect the human features around them?

■ *Part of the Himalayas are in northern India.*

Activity

1 Look at the photograph below of the area around Chembakolli.

2 Is the landscape hilly or flat?

3 Are there any trees, rivers, or swamps?

4 Think about the main physical and human features of the area, and how they might affect each other.

What are the homes of the children like?

We can find out more about the homes in a **settlement** by asking these questions:

- What materials are the houses made of? What are the reasons for this?
- How much time do people spend in their homes?
- What happens in the home? (for example, cooking, sleeping, or leisure)
- How many people share the same house?
- What are the houses like inside? Are there several rooms?
- Do the houses have running water and electricity?

■ *These houses in the UK are made from stone and the roofs are thatched.*

Homes in Chembakolli

The **weather** in Chembakolli changes depending on the time of year. Sometimes it is wet. Sometimes it is wet. Sometimes it is dry and hot, or dry and cold! Houses have overhanging roofs to create shade from the sun and protection from the rain.

In Chembakolli the houses have only two or three rooms for everyone in the family to live in. There are mostly three or four children in each family, plus the adults. During the day, the family will not spend much time in the house, as it would be very crowded.

Rural Indian homes do not have many of the facilities we have. It is unusual to find indoor toilets, televisions, washing machines, or refrigerators. In Chembakolli there is no electricity or clean running water piped into the houses. The women collect water from wells. They have to carry the water up a steep hill from the well to their home. Can you imagine having to collect and carry home all the water you use in a day?

■ *This house in Chembakolli is made from dried soil and mud. Its thatched roof is made using plants from the nearby forest.*

Activity

Make a chart of the similarities and differences that you can think of between your house and a child's house in Chembakolli. Use the questions on the opposite page as headings in your chart to help you.

What is the school like?

Much of your day is spent at school. There will be some subjects in school that you enjoy and others that you do not enjoy as much. You are lucky to be able to go to school and study the subjects you do. In India some children are not able to go to school at all.

■ *This school in the UK has plenty of space and good facilities for the children.*

A busy school

There is no school in Chembakolli. Children from Chembakolli go to a primary school in Gudalar, which is 15 miles (24 kilometeres) away. They travel to school by jeep which takes an hour each way. Most children do not go to secondary school.

Children from Chembakolli study many of the subjects that you do, like maths, english, science, geography, and history. They also study Tamil and local music and crafts. The children are taught in large classes of around 40 pupils.

Some children in the village do not go to school at all. This is because their families need them to help with work in the fields, or by looking after younger brothers and sisters. Also, many parents do not see the point of sending their children to school, because when they leave they will go back to working in the fields, just as they did and their parents did before them.

Activity

The school in Gudalar is probably very different to your school. Write down all the similarities and differences you can think of.

Exploring further

On the Heinemann Explore website or CD-ROM go to Exploring > Villages. Read the article 'Raipole – human aspects' and find out how a day in the life of a child in Raipole in India compares with a day in your life.

What is the main type of work?

In geography we learn about how the **physical features** of the **landscape** have a direct effect on how people live. Often they also affect the kinds of jobs that people do in the area. For example, if a **settlement** is near the sea, many of the people may be fishermen.

Farming in Chembakolli

Most people in Chembakolli are farmers. Their fields are just outside the village. They grow many different crops, including tea, bananas, pineapples, mangoes and peppercorns. The farming is done by hand, not with machinery, as the farms are small. The whole family works in the fields, including the children. Families must work very hard to make sure they produce enough food to eat and still have some left over to sell.

■ *Growing tea is very important in the area around Chembakolli.*

Selling and trading goods

The farmers of Chembakolli may not be able to grow all the food they need, so they trade some of what they grow for other types of food. They take their produce to a market nearby. If they have bullocks they can use them to transport their produce to market. Some people travel a long way to buy or trade goods at a market. It may be the only place where they can find some of the things they need to live.

■ *Look closely at this market in India. Can you see what sort of goods are being bought and sold?*

Activity

Answer the following questions about farming in Chembakolli.

1 Which types of crops are grown in Chembakolli?

2 What methods of farming are used?

3 What do you think happens to the crops once they are harvested?

Glossary

aerial photograph   picture taken from the air

atlas   book of maps

bullock   young bull

capital city   a country's most important city. It is usually where the government is based.

city   large town

continent   one of the main masses of land in the world

delta   fan-shaped area at the mouth of a river. It is made up of solid material that is left by the river as it enters the sea.

desert   large area of very dry, often sandy land

enclosure   fenced-off piece of land

fertile   soil that is good for growing crops

fortified   strengthened against enemies or danger

grid reference   position marked by numbering the squares on a map

hamlet   settlement that is made up of just a few houses

harbour   sheltered area of water where boats and ships can safely stay when they are not at sea

headland   area of land that juts out into the sea

human features   all the things in a place made by humans, such as housing, factories, and roads

isolated settlement   single house or farm

key   panel to explain the features on a map or graph

landscape   scenery and its features

mangrove   group of low trees with exposed roots, usually found in tropical swamps

manufacturing   making objects, especially in a factory

meander   bend in a river

mineral   hard substance that can be dug out of the ground, such as coal

nature reserve   an area where natural life is conserved

outskirts outer border or edge of a settlement

paddy farming growing rice

physical features natural features of a place, such as rivers, hills, and woodlands

plantation large farm producing one crop

population how many people live in a place

rural in the countryside

secondary sources reference books such as encyclopedias and the Internet

settlement place where people live

town large area with many streets, houses, shops, offices and businesses where people live and work

village small settlement that is made up of houses and services, such as a pub or post office

water meadow field that is sometimes flooded by a stream or river

weather rain, snow, sunshine, cloud, and wind at a particular time or place

Find out more

Books
Mapping the UK: Mapping settlements, Louise Spilsbury (Heinemann Library, 2005)
Chembakolli: Life and change in an Indian village, Helen Day (Actionaid, 2002)
Village life in India, Steve Brace, (Cambridge University Press, 2002)

Websites
www.chembakolli.com
This website is packed full of information and photographs on Chembakolli.

www.heinemannexplore.com
Check out the settlements section of the Heinemann Explore website to find out more about different types of settlements including towns, cities, seaside resorts and villages. You can also see lots of interactive maps and videos.

Index